OCCASIONAL CONTRIBUTIONS FROM THE MUSEUM OF
ANTHROPOLOGY OF THE UNIVERSITY OF MICHIGAN
NO. 4

THE SACRED EDIFICES OF
THE BATAK OF SUMATRA

BY

HARLEY HARRIS BARTLETT

ANN ARBOR, MICHIGAN
UNIVERSITY OF MICHIGAN PRESS
July 5, 1934

© 1934 by the Regents of the University of Michigan
The Museum of Anthropology
All rights reserved

ISBN (print): 978-1-949098-59-4
ISBN (ebook): 978-1-951538-59-0

Browse all of our books at
sites.lsa.umich.edu/archaeology-books.

Order our books from the University of Michigan
Press at www.press.umich.edu.

For permissions, questions, or manuscript queries,
contact Museum publications by email at umma-pubs@umich.edu or visit the Museum website at
lsa.umich.edu/ummaa.

CONTENTS

	PAGE
PARSOEROAN (Pardembanan and Simeloengoen)	1
DJORO (Toba), *DJERAT* (Pardembanan, Simeloengoen, and Karo), *PĚNDAWANĚN* and *GĚRITĚN* (Karo)	11
PANTANGĚN (Karo)	16
ANDJAPAN (Pardembanan), *BĚBERĚN* and *ANDJAP-ANDJAP* (Karo), *LANGGATAN* (Toba)	17

Notes on Related Matters

Unburied Coffins	21
Equestrian Figures	21
Stone Sarcophagi and Gravestones Shaped Like Sarcophagi	26
References	29
Plates I-XXXI with Descriptions	*facing* 31

THE SACRED EDIFICES OF THE BATAK OF SUMATRA[1]

THE chief object of this article is to make a record of certain sacred and ceremonial structures that were formerly characteristic of the Batak region of Sumatra, namely, the *parsoeroan* (temple) of Asahan and Simeloengoen, the *djoro* (grave shrine) of Toba, and the *djerat* (grave house) of Simeloengoen. Secondarily, there are short notes on sarcophagi, ceremonial and magical inclosures, and ceremonial apparatus (such as altars) that are of such bulky or temporary nature as not to be represented in ordinary ethnographic collections. Of these a photographic record must take the place of museum specimens. The chief of these are the *langgatan* of Toba, the *bĕbĕren* and *andjap-andjap* of Karoland, and the *andjapan* of Asahan.

PARSOEROAN (PARDEMBANAN AND SIMELOENGOEN)

The *parsoeroan* is the temple of the pagan Pardembanan Batak of Asahan and the Timoer Batak of Tano Djawa, Simeloengoen. As has elsewhere been pointed out (4), this region is characterized by the type of symbolic grave-post known as the *anisan* and by the grave house known as the *djerat*. The *anisan* does not extend farther north into Simeloengoen, so far as the writer has been able to discover, or south of the Asahan River, or into the highlands of Toba. It is a surviving element of an intrusive culture, possibly from the eastern coast of Middle or South Sumatra, and evidently pre-Islamic, that merged with the culture of the

---

[1] Paper from the Department of Botany, University of Michigan, No. 419. Presented at the thirty-third annual meeting of the Michigan Academy, in 1928.

highland Batak as the latter spread into the lowlands with colonizing groups from Toba.

In lowland Asahan not much of either the true Batak culture or the putative intrusive culture has survived the impacts of Islam and the European plantation system during the last couple of generations. The vestiges of sacred inclosures containing permanently maintained sanctuaries are disappearing rapidly or may have even disappeared in the last few years. These equivalents of temples, together with certain characteristic grave structures, constitute the most obvious features of what the writer has termed the intrusive element in the paganism of the Pardembanan region of Asahan and the adjacent Simeloengoen district of Tano Djawa.

In speaking of a Batak temple, one immediately lays himself open to a charge of faulty interpretation or superficial observation. Warneck (24), the chief student of Batak religion, came to the considered conclusion that the Batak have no temples. Even for the mountain people there is evidence that he should have qualified his statement. As to the lowland peoples of the East Coast, generally quite disregarded by writers on the Batak, the Pardembanan group in Asahan and part of the Timoer or Simeloengoen Batak (those of Tano Djawa) had the *parsoeroan*, a house for the spirits within a permanently maintained *parhordjaan* (sacred inclosure), served by a priest, and certainly the equivalent of a temple. In a previous paper referring to the Batak of lowland Asahan, it has been shown that beating the drums at the *parsoeroan* to summon the spirits was one of the established duties of the *datoe* (magician-priest).

The diminutive *parsoeroan* was not itself a place of assembly, for it was too small to hold more than six or eight adults. It was never entered except when the *datoe* put it in order in preparation for ceremonies, placed offerings within it, or removed the latter after the spirits were supposed to have consumed the *tondi* (soul stuff) of the offerings.

It was therefore the sacred inclosure, in conjunction with the sanctuary, that made up the equivalent of a temple. The inclosure itself was never violated by non-ceremonial uses. It was not trespassed upon, and before it was used as a place of assembly for ceremonies, the *datoe* took precautions to purify the people as they entered, in order that they might not be accompanied within the inclosure by evil spirits. He also carried out an elaborate preliminary purificatory ceremony in order to exorcise any uninvited evil spirits that might have entered in spite of such magical protective devices as hanging fringes and the crossed sticks known as *silang*.

The *parsoeroan* contained no permanent furniture except a *parasapan* (censer) and a *pinggan* (big plate). In the former gum benzoin was burned on ceremonial occasions, when offerings of food were placed upon the plate. The entrance was veiled by a hanging cloth, which was kept in order by the *datoe*. The *parsoeroan* was placed at right angles to the house of the chief and its entrance faced east. In construction it was a small replica of the middle room of a chief's great house.

Underneath it were benches on which ancestral spirits and gods were believed to rest. Here were frequently stored the sacred gongs and drums (Pl. VIII, Fig. 1), the ones used for ordinary festivities being kept in the house of the chief. North (always?) of the *parsoeroan* but within the sacred inclosure was erected the *andjapan* (altar, Pl. IV), which was renewed each time that important ceremonies were to be held. The *andjapan* has been discussed and figured in a former article (5). Somewhere near or under the *parsoeroan* was a hollowed stone called the *batoe paranggiran* (Pl. VII, Fig. 2), in which were placed portions of the purifying liquids and the peelings of the purifying limes, used upon occasions of ceremonial purification. An account of such a ceremony has been given elsewhere (5, pp. 14–18; 16, pp. 16–17). It seems that in general the offerings placed in the *batoe paranggiran* were fragrant or strongly odorous. When the stone was not in use it was covered over with earth or with palm leaves, or mats, and it could be uncovered only by the *datoe*.

The *parhordjaan* (place of ceremonies) around the *parsoeroan* was either inclosed by a permanent stockade (Pls. I, VI–VII) or a light fence (Pl. III), which was not allowed to fall into complete disrepair in the intervals between ceremonies, and was invariably restored and provided with new *gaba-gaba* (fringes) made of the still yellow, not yet unfolded, leaflets of the sugar palm, whenever ceremonies were to be held.

There was not necessarily a *parsoeroan* in the district of each chief. Even some of the more important chiefs built a temporary inclosure around the big house when there were to be ceremonies. Within this inclosure the altar was built and beside it a structure of palm thatch under which the gongs were hung and beside which the *borotan* (sacrificial post) was erected.

Not the least interesting feature of the permanent ceremonial inclosure surrounding the *parsoeroan* was that here were planted the various sacred and protective plants, such as the generally odorous or highly colored (red or yellow) herbs known as *roedang*, the aromatic plants known as *hosea*, and the narcotic plants *pining* (betel-nut palm), *demban* (pepper vine), and *tembaho* (tobacco). Some of these plants were not always sacred and when grown in the sacred inclosure were, therefore, specifically dedicated to the gods. Here also were fruit trees and coco palms dedicated to the gods, and the curious little palm, *andoedoer (Caryota furfuracea)*, from which palm wine is prepared only to be offered to the spirits. For human beings it is made from Arenga, the sugar palm (3).

The change in native customs that has come about in the last few years is quite astonishing. In 1918 there were very few *parsoeroan* left, and the writer made it somewhat of a hobby to visit and photograph, if possible, each one of which he heard. Most of the photographs presented with this article date from 1918. By 1927 so great had been the change that only one *parsoeroan* was seen. It was in a little village reserve (Kampong Taratak) surrounded by the great Tindjoan oil-palm concession in Tano Djawa. The natives refused to tell where it was, but by hunting diligently, fording a deep river, and finally subsidizing a small boy, the writer found it. The fence was gone, but a hen had been sacrificed under the building within a day or two, showing that it was still used.

If there is scientific value in making a record of fast disappearing ethnographic details, the notes and photographs of the *parsoeroan* herewith presented are indeed precious. They prove the existence of a Batak temple, which has been said not to exist, and for the East Coast region there will presumably never be any addition to this record. The pagans of the lowland are about gone. The writer has taken great pains to see all he could that is of ethnological importance in Asahan, and nothing more interesting or distinctive than the *parsoeroan* has been found.

The statement that the Batak have no priests, no temples, and no idols was made by Waitz (22) in his popular *Anthropologie der Naturvölker* and gained wide acceptance from this source, which was not, of course, original. He merely quoted Junghuhn (10, p. 249), one of the first to visit the Batak, who in 1847 had said:

> Aerzte übrigens haben sie ebenso wenig wie Priester, Tempel ebenso wenig wie Hospitaler, und von einer Religionsdoctrin eben so wenig eine Spur, als von einem Kultus odor von einem Idol, das sie verehrten.

The first more accurate statement was made by Hagen (7), who in 1883, on a scientific trip to the northeastern extremity of Toba Lake, made observations at Naga Sariboe, where he stayed, just within the border of the Simeloengoen region. Here he found two kinds of religious structures, one of them a small house similar to a grave house but rising on four posts, like an ordinary dwelling, some fifteen feet above the ground. It stood near the *bale-bale* (guest house and men's social center) and was dedicated to the protective spirit of the village. It was in bad repair, and not carefully maintained. This record of Hagen's appears to be the only definite mention of such a structure in the literature, and there is no reason to doubt its entire authenticity. Whether or not a structure dedicated to a protective spirit is to be regarded as a temple depends upon one's definition of a temple. At any rate Hagen's observation has been neglected.

In 1894 Pleyte (14, p. 45) wrote:

> Temples with images of the gods one seeks in vain in the Bataklands. Only Si Singa Mangaradja, one of the forefathers of the present chief of this name, seems to have possessed in olden times a sort of sanctuary in which the faithful assembled in order to serve and worship him. However, the reports regarding this structure are so vague that it is impossible to establish at a later date anything regarding the arrangement and appearance of it. It can only be ascertained that now it no longer exists. For the gods as well as for the spirits there have never existed true temples, certainly not, it would seem, since the Hindu period. The few ruins from that period found scattered here and there in the Batak lands suggest both by their measurements and form, prayer chapels, and not churches in any sense.

The grave houses which are commonly found in Simeloengoen, Asahan, and Toba are not usually given the status of temples by writers on Batak religion. Since they are places where the ancestral spirits are worshiped, and where offerings are made, it would seem that their small size and restricted importance (each *djerat* or *djoro* being

SACRED EDIFICES OF SUMATRA 7

resorted to only by the relatives of the person buried there), and the fact that they are not regularly attended by a priest, may well exclude them from the category of temples. With regard to this point, however, the most thorough student of Batak religion has held two opinions. In 1906 Warneck (23) defined *djoro* as "a house that is not inhabited by human beings, but has a specified purpose"; *bagas djoro* as:

> A house of the dead, such as they like to build on the graves of outstanding chiefs, also a temple, for the use of making offerings;

and *djoro ni onan,* as "a little house for offerings which stands at the market place." Later, in 1909, he wrote (24):

> *Djoro,* a little house that is erected on the market place and at stem festivities as a temporary abode of an ancestor. Moreover the little structures exactly similar to a Batak house are so named, that are erected over the graves of notable chiefs. Both, however, are not temples, but temporary media of worship. There is no temple among the Batak.

So much for the positive statements that are prominent in the literature. They refer to Toba and Simeloengoen and to Bakkara, the former seat of the Batak priest kings (Si Singa Mangaradja) in the northwestern part of the Toba region. Since the southern Batak lands (Padang Lawas, Mandailing, and Angkola) have been so largely Muhammadan for a long time, it can hardly be expected that pagan religious structures will still be reported from that region. Joustra (9) mentions that there are peculiar religious schools in the southern Muhammadan Batak lands known as *soero*. The word base is of course the same as in *parsoeroan*. Is such a school perhaps a survival from pagan days—a sacred inclosure with its building appropriated to the propagation of Islam? Joustra says that the *soero* in the southern Batak lands is a sleeping place for the young men and boys, as well as a religious school, which fact would seem to indicate that it is now of a very different nature from the *parsoeroan* even if formerly the same. Its present significance may have been derived, with Islam, from the Minangkabo people to the south. In this connection it may be remarked that the word also persists in the Malay Peninsula as *surau*, "a private chapel, in contradistinction to a mosque of general assembly" (26, p. 647). Is the Peninsular *surau* also a relic of the pre-Islamic religion of the Malay, anciently propagated from Middle Sumatra? Among the Minangkabo of Sumatra there is the same use of *soerau* in the sense of "school or private chapel" (17, p. 57). Commonly, the *soerau* in Middle Sumatra pertains to a *hadji* who there gathers the youths about him to teach them to write. Many chiefs have *soerau* where they pray and sometimes offer opportunity for religious instruction. The larger ones are hardly to be distinguished from mosques.

That in Middle Sumatra, the cradle of Malay culture, Islam may have found and appropriated a preëxisting religious structure, the *soerau*, to its own use is perhaps indicated by the following facts: (1) In both the mosques and *soerau* of Middle Sumatra, according to Van Hasselt (17, p. 57), the call to prayer is by drum. He says that the minaret, from which in other Muhammadan countries the faithful are called to prayer, is lacking, but in place of it one sees in the Padang Highlands and in Rawas great drums, called *bedoek* or *taboew*, from which the calls to prayer are issued. (2) Sometimes, at least, drums used only for summoning important assemblies were kept in special small structures, carved and ornamented, one of which, at Alahanpandjang, is beautifully illustrated by Van Hasselt (18, p. 25, Pl. LXIV, Fig. 5). Such a structure in size and architecture reminds one strongly of the *parsoeroan*. (3) It is the tradition in Asahan (5, p. 38) that one of the chief duties of the *datoe* or pagan priest was to beat the drum at the *parsoeroan* as a call for the assembly of the gods and ancestral spirits to whom offerings were to be made and prayers addressed. One can hardly avoid the strong suspicion that the *soerau*, as a place of ceremonial drumming, was an element of pre-Islamic Middle Sumatran Malay culture, that it came to Asahan and Tano Djawa from the Malays, and is one of the elements of an old intrusive culture which reached and affected especially the lowland Batak of the Pardembanan and Simeloengoen groups.

Negative evidence does not have the value of positive, but it is at least indicative of the rarity of religious buildings in the northern Batak lands that in well-known Karoland nothing that can be called such has been described except the *gĕritĕn* (ancestral skull house), at which there are religious ceremonies consisting of prayers and offerings to the ancestors. The *pantangĕn* of the *goeroe* (teacher) or *datoe* (magician) seems to be magical rather than primarily religious.

A long discussion of what a temple is or is not would hardly be profitable here. In considering the *parsoeroan* of Asahan and Tano Djawa as the equivalent of a temple, the writer wishes to emphasize these points: (1) It was a place for the greater religious observances that concerned all the people subject to the chief in whose village it was maintained; (2) it was a permanent structure; (3) it was holy and was not desecrated by any common use; (4) it was dedicated to the gods and deified ancestors; (5) it was under the care of the chief *datoe*; (6) although the small building itself was not a place of assembly, being more in the nature of a holy of holies, to be entered only by the *datoe*, it was generally surrounded by a permanent sacred inclosure which was a place of assembly for the participants in ceremonies. Surely there are here some points of contrast to the conception voiced by Pleyte (14) as follows:

> In the past as well as now the Batak has worshipped his gods in the open air or in his dwelling; the open field, the village

street and his house were and are still today the places where he offers to them. Only the *sombaon* was reverenced in its wide wood.

An objection to such unqualified statements as these should be made because the religion of the Batak has been used in the *Quellen der Religions-Geschichte* (24) as a "paradigm for the animistic religions of the Indian Archipelago." If there are wide variations of religious theory and practice among the Batak themselves, as in the matter of the idea of the multiple soul versus unformed soul stuff, for instance, and the maintenance of a temple, these deviations from the paradigm should receive due consideration, even though the deviation (as in the example of the *parsoeroan*) may possibly indicate ancient pre-Islamic influence from the Minangkabo region.

The word *parsoeroan*, from the word base, *soero*, means place of invocation. *Soero* has been considered Common Indonesian, and extends beyond Indonesia at least to Fiji (11). With the coming of Islam, Arabic words were used for things pertaining to the new religion, and the persistence of *surau* in the sense of "a religious edifice" is a good indication that there was a pre-Islamic pagan structure to which the word applied. The structure sometimes lingers in regions that have gone over to Islam as a pagan survival side by side with the *mesdjid* ("mosque"), and the name for it still persists, but rarely, in old tales.

Aside from presumably Indonesian *surau*, Malay has the word *surah* in the sense of "pray," "ask aid," or "demand." Javanese has the same word. It seems to be an adoption of the Arabic word for the Muslim confession of faith, only accidentally similar to *soero* and its cognates, unless there is really some truth in the theory several times advanced that there is a large, pre-Islamic, Semitic element in the Oceanic languages.

In Asahan three variations of Indonesian *soero* are heard, namely, *soero, soeroe,* and *soeroeng,* the last being the peculiar attention-compelling vocative form which is used in the invocations to the *pagar* and *pangoeloebalang,* by which the *datoe* compels the captive spirit to exert its protective or destructive power. (Scores of inscribed bamboo joints in the writer's collection of Batak manuscripts are such invocations, beginning with the powerful word *soeroeng.*) Sundanese has *soroh,* Old Javanese, *sereh,* Karo, *soero;* and many other equivalents could be brought forward. The Fiji *soro* is exceptionally interesting because it is used in a country so far to the east. It means "to beg forgiveness," "an atonement." Kubary (11[a]) described with fine colored plates structures similar to the Batak *parsoeroan* as far from Sumatra as the Palau Islands. Hernsheim (7,[a]) Pl. 5) shows a fine example in one of his colored lithographs. Matsumura (12[a]) describes a shrine at Koror, Palau, as:

> .... a club house in miniature, being about 1 by 2 mm. It has simple carvings on the outside, but has no idol or image of a deity, though it is a place of worship. (Plate XXXI.)

Some of the *parsoeroan* observed were in villages where no dwelling house constructed according to the Batak tradition still existed. The sacred nature of the temple demanded, however, that it follow the old type of architecture, and Plates I–VIII show how careful the construction was.

DJORO (TOBA), DJERAT (PARDEMBANAN, SIMELOENGOEN, AND KARO), PĔNDAWANĚN AND GĔRITĔN (KARO)

The two types of ceremonial *djoro* of the Toba Batak have already been mentioned. One, the temporary ceremonial house erected at a market place, the writer does not happen to have seen.[2] The other, a miniature house erected

---

[2] One of the important Dairi ceremonies which involved the erection of this first type of *djoro* is described by Ypes (27, p. 171). His book is a

over the grave of an important man, used as a place for making offerings to his spirit, is still characteristic of the Toba landscape in pagan neighborhoods, but, notwithstanding the extensive literature on Batak ethnology, it has never had more than casual mention. In a former paper (4, p. 3) the writer alluded to the Toba word *djoro* as being possibly related to Simeloengoen *djerat* (Arabic *ziarat*), but also noted the similarity to Balinese *djero* (house). It appears that the latter word is a true cognate of *djoro*, and that the verbal resemblance to *djerat*, striking because both words refer to a structure built over a grave, may be accidental.³ We may infer, from the fact that *djerat* is a word used by Muhammadans for the graves of unbelievers, and also by the pagans themselves without any feeling that it is an undignified term, or one that casts any reproach upon them, that it was introduced by Arabic contact in the pre-Islamic period.⁴ The pre-Islamic Batak word for a shrine over the grave of a distinguished man is *parsimangotan* (the "place of the *simangot*" or deified ancestral spirit). *Djerat* is, to be sure, a more general term, but spirits were classified into more categories by pagans than by Muhammadans, and the nomenclature of the abodes of spirits was correspondingly more precise.

mine of valuable information about matters which are insufficiently treated by other writers. Dealing as it does with the Dairi, about whom too little has been published, it fills an especially great gap in the literature.

³ Another verbal similarity which may be more than accidental, and which will bear looking into, in connection with the linguistic evidence of early cultural borrowings by Sumatra from India, is between *djerat*, *djirat*, and *jira*, in Sikhim the name of the two emblematic umbrellas on a temple. See L. A. Waddell, in *Gazetteer of Sikhim*, Calcutta: Bengal Secretariat Press, 1894, p. 260).

⁴Maass (12, pp. 153–212) gives two examples of the persistence of the grave house and of the word, in the form *djirè*, in Central Sumatra, where the Malay (not Batak) population has long been entirely Muhammadan. In one instance the term is used to refer to the elaborate and beautiful little grave house, in the Minangkabo style of architecture, on the grave of an uncle of the Sultan of Siak at Goenoeng Sahilan. The other is at Boekit Sa-baleh, and also has the complex horn-gabled roofs which are best known in the Padang Highlands of West Sumatra.

The *djoro* (Pls. IX–XIV) is a Toba structure and resembles a house in every detail. It has house carvings and painting in red, white, and black, and is elevated on posts. The *djerat* is its equivalent in the Pardembanan and Tano Djawa districts. Of the illustrations that have been published one (4, Pl. XIV) is altogether typical. Another (4, Pl. VI) represents a structure more elaborate than usual, with greater height above the floor, and a third (4, Pl. XVI) is elevated on the top of a granary in order that the harvest may have the immediate protection of the ancestral spirits. Only one such elaborate structure was seen. A typical *djerat* (Pl. XV, Fig. 1) looks houselike on account of the sloping swaybacked roof, but the only inclosed chamber with vertical walls is at the ground level. It has posts which serve as corners into which the horizontal railings that make up the walls are mortised, or to which they are tied if, as is usually true, the horizontal poles or rails inclosing the graves are laid in alternate pairs, a pair of side rails lengthwise crossed by a pair of end rails crosswise, and so on. There is only height enough to clear the grave-posts. Then a floor of poles or rails is laid crosswise, each piece being tightly tied into notches in the uppermost pair of side rails. Directly above this floor is the sloping roof, that is, there is no upper chamber with walls, corresponding to the elevated house. The ordinary *djerat* is merely a strongly built cratelike structure of crossed rails, protecting the grave furniture, and covered by a roof. One finds that whenever the relatives of the dead have gone to the trouble of making a *djerat*, there will be a correct grave with one or more carved grave-posts within it. The *djerat* is most common in Tano Djawa, where frequently the male and female forms of the grave-post are found on the same grave (Pl. XV, Figs. 2–3). In Asahan it was used rarely, and only for chiefs' graves; the distinction between male and female posts was always observed. In those parts of

Toba where the *djoro,* a complete miniature house, is built over the grave, the writer has not seen it used in conjunction with any post whatever, unless a small post sometimes placed at the center of the roof (Pl. XII, Fig. 2) represents the grave-post.

In the Pardembanan district (Asahan) the grave may or may not be near the dwelling house. If it is not, the location is often that of other, older graves, near which a dwelling once stood. In Tano Djawa the graves are frequently in the village, among the houses and at right angles to them. In Toba the burial place is outside the village, often on a hill, where the newer graves of important people are marked by *djoro,* in all stages of disrepair, and the older graves only by clumps of lemon grass—in Toba an almost invariable accompaniment of a grave (see Pl. IX, Fig. 2).

More particular details of both *djoro* and *djerat* may be found in the descriptions of Plates IX–XVI. There is much about the accessories and ornamentation of the *djoro* that needs elucidation, but the writer has never stayed long enough in the Toba districts to get dependable information. Others who might have done so have disregarded the structures almost completely. There is decided interest among Europeans in Batak *ethnographica* which can be collected, but very little in larger things such as houses, graves, etc., which can be only described and photographed.

The mortuary customs of Karoland are more diverse than those of the other Batak districts. The *mĕrga* Sĕmbiring burns its dead, and, at intervals of years, festivals are held during which the bones remaining are placed in *pĕrahoe ngombak* (miniature boats) and floated down the Lao Biang. A *goeroe* of this *mĕrga* is not burned, however, and members of other *mĕrga* are burned under some circumstances, although no one seems to have made inquiries to find out exactly when and why. Ordinarily a body is buried, and the *pĕndawanĕn* (burial place) is surrounded by a bamboo fence, within which are grown many kinds of sacred plants, always including *kalindjoehang (Cordyline fruticosa)*. The grave is covered by a very neatly made little house *(roemah-roemah; djerat)*, which, for an ordinary man, resembles the *djerat* of Simeloengoen or the *djoro* of Toba in that the roof has a single lengthwise gable, like the *roemah galoeh* of the village. The grave house of a *sibajak* (chief) is frequently built with crossed gables, and with a *pajoeng* or an *andjoeng-andjoeng* (an umbrella- or a steeple-like structure) surmounting the center, so that it resembles the *roemah tersek*, the most elaborate house type of the village (Pl. XVI, Fig. 1). The *roemah tersek* is generally, as are also some of the single-gabled houses (Pl. XIX, Fig. 1), surmounted by a miniature house, which is also called *andjoeng-andjoeng*. Beside the grave is a tall bamboo pole with a magical device of bamboo or pleated palm leaves hanging from it. This serves as a *pandji* ("flag") by which the spirit of the deceased recognizes his place.

It is customary to open the graves of chiefs, after the bodies have decayed, and to remove the skulls. These are carefully cleaned, decorated with gold and silver ornaments, wrapped in cloths, and then preserved in the village in a special building called the *gĕritĕn*. The *gĕritĕn* at Kaban Djahe, containing the skulls of the ancestors of Pa Melga, a former chief, was opened for Adam (1) so that he might photograph the skulls. It is built like a small *roemah tersek* (see Pl. XVI, Fig. 2). It was, in 1918, surrounded by a low woven fence of split bamboo, which has since disappeared, but will doubtless be renewed on the occasion of further ceremonies. The fence marked off the area sacred to the ancestral spirits, and corresponded to the *parhordjaan* of Asahan and Tano Djawa, which has been referred to in the discussion of the *parsoeroan*. It was constructed in just the same manner as that of the *bĕbĕren (bĕrebĕren)* of which a description follows (p. 17). After being preserved a number of generations the skulls are said to be cremated.

Although at Kaban Djahe the *gĕritĕn* is a structure of considerable size, it is in many instances, according to Von Brenner (20), a diminutive model of a dwelling house, about four feet in length. Within is a wooden coffin, usually boat-shaped, beautifully carved and painted, in which the exhumed skull and larger bones of the dead man are preserved. Such small bone houses were seen by Von Brenner in 1887 singly or in groups in any part of the Karo villages. One which he figures (20, p. 28) has the form of an ordinary *parpagaran* (conical receptacle for offerings, made by splitting into several sticks and spreading out the end joint of a bamboo pole), except that it is covered by a conical roof. At Kampong Kĕling there was in 1918 a very small *gĕritĕn*, in the form of the simplest house type.

PANTANGĚN (KARO)

Joustra (9, p. 120) merely mentions the Karo *pantangĕn* as the place where the *goeroe* studies and gives lessons. He supposes it to be the equivalent of the Simeloengoen structure known as *anggoenan*. The writer has not seen the latter, but had the interesting experience of visiting a fine Karo *pantangĕn*, that of Goeroe (Datoe) na Bolon, at the foot of Dĕlĕng Koetoe near Kampong Goersinga (Pl. XVII). It is a square inclosure surrounded by a double hedge with a maze entrance, so as to be entirely private. It is *pantang* ("forbidden"), the Batak equivalent of *tabu*, to all except those whom the *goeroe* invites to enter. The house is only large enough for the *goeroe* to occupy along with his magical and ceremonial apparatus. It is guarded by a stone *pangoeloebalang* and a large stuffed snake. The *pantangĕn* is not dedicated to the gods and ancestral spirits as is the *parsoeroan* in Asahan. Its use is magical rather than religious, and of course, it is not in any sense a temple.

It is kept scrupulously neat and tidy. The little house contains drums, gongs, the masks for the *topeng-koeda-koeda* dance, *pĕrminakĕn* (containers for magical mixtures), and various other paraphernalia of the magician.

ANDJAPAN (PARDEMBANAN), *BĔBĔREN* AND
ANDJAP-ANDJAP (KARO), *LANGGATAN* (TOBA)

The several Batak districts have somewhat similar types of altar on which, or within which, offerings are made to the spirits. The *andjapan* of the Pardembanan group in Asahan has already been described and illustrated (5, Pls. V–VII). It varies in elaborateness according to the importance of the spirits invoked, the number of persons participating in the ceremony, and the nature of the ceremonies. It has a counterpart in the other Batak districts. In Karoland the simplest possible type of a small table-like support (often of bamboo) serves for the offerings of fruits, *sirih*, etc., and is known as *andjap-andjap*. In places supposedly haunted by wild spirits, where man is a trespasser, no inclosure is built around it. A visitor to the crater of the volcano Dĕlĕng Sibajak will nearly always find at the rim above the crater lake a fresh *andjap-andjap* (Pl. XXI) on which are offerings, and old broken down ones are always to be seen.

In the Karo kampongs one of the most frequent sights is a little square or round sacred inclosure, the fence of which is made of pleated split bamboo or similar material. It is only eight or ten feet across, and is known as the *bĕbĕren* (*bĕrebĕren*, "place for making offerings"). Within this inclosure (Pls. XVIII–XX), the *andjap-andjap* is generally erected. If a visitor asks about it he is usually told that it is *tempat tĕndi* ("a place for souls"). Ypes (27) has recently shown, in one of the finest contributions to the ethnology of the East Indies ever made, that the Pakpak subdivision of the Dairi Batak, who are neighbors of the

Karo on the west, and their closest relatives, also have a soul place in their villages. It is located in the center of the village site, and is called the *toenggoeng*, the dwelling place of the *tĕndi* (soul) of the village. When the village was founded a suitable place was chosen and a ceremony carried out to ascertain that the omens were auspicious. A bamboo receptacle filled with water was set up in the ground, and next to it a *pĕnalĕpĕn* (summoner of spirits) consisting of a wand, cleft at the top to hold a *sirih* leaf. (See Pl. XX, Fig. 2 for the corresponding Karo device, called *pĕrsĕmbahĕn*.) Next to it was placed a piece of banana leaf with an offering of *bĕras bani* (rice) upon it. After prayers were offered to the spirits to favor the establishment of the new village, the apparatus was left until the next morning. If the bamboo was still full the omens were good. If it had run over (by condensation of dew) the omens were especially good. Then the spot where the bamboo had been was set aside for the *toenggoeng*, which was henceforth considered to be the habitation of the soul of the village. The Karo *bĕbĕren* is undoubtedly closely similar to the round Pakpak *toenggoeng*, as its frequently circular shape would seem to indicate. Although the *bĕbĕren* may be either round or square, every other ceremonial structure seen in the Batak lands by the writer was rectangular, and the Dairi Batak (Simsim group especially) seem to be the only Batak group in which a round ground plan for a village or large structure is ever seen.

The *toenggoeng*, like the *bĕbĕren*, is planted with ceremonial or sacred plants. Ypes names, for the *toenggoeng*, banana, *silindjoeang (Cordyline fruticosa)*, *sangka simpilit*, and *babar sĕmah*. (Some plant or other called *soma* or *sĕmah* is especially important in the ceremonies of each Batak group, and probably it is reminiscent of the Indic *homa*.) The *bĕbĕren* may have a considerable variety of plants in it and if so *kalindjoehang (Cordyline fruticosa)* is nearly always most conspicuous. There may be a banana plant, a collection of diverse *Codiaea* with brightly colored leaves, and a variety of *roedang* (aromatic plants or plants with red flowers). The best discussion of the *bĕbĕren* is that of Neumann (13), who does not, however, illustrate it.

In the Toba districts the altar is called *langgatan*. It is becoming rare because of the influence of Christianity, but may still be found in Habinsaran, where most of the Batak are still *parbegoe* (spirit worshipers). A *langgatan* found beside a path near Hoeta Godang, Habinsaran, was essentially the two-storied *andjapan* of Asahan, except that it was simpler in construction. The lower compartment had only a sparse fringe of shredded palm leaflets for side walls. The upper compartment was the usual high-peaked, dense thatch of palm leaves, but was altogether open at the front. Leading up to it was the *belatoek dopak toroe* (notched-pole ladder), with the notches upside down (as in Asahan—see Pl. XXXI, and also 5, Pl. XI), indicating that it was to be visited by upside-down spirits. Since the structure was small, the larger *pinang* (betel-nut palm) inflorescences which were exposed as offerings hung, not on the *langgatan* itself, but on a little frame at the left side of the front (the observer's right as he faced the *langgatan*). The offerings within the upper compartment were as follows (names given in the sub-Toba dialect of the locality):

pinang tikiltikilan (young Areca inflorescence)
demban tikiltikilan (unripe Areca nut)
pege (ginger)
sanggoel (a bouquet of leaves made up as if to be worn in the hair, but used in some ceremonies to asperge a purificatory liquid)
tambis (branches of a plant especially attractive to spirits. It is said that the spirits of Toba will not visit an altar which does not contain *tambis*, or favor a locality where it does not grow)

parboewe (rice)

The lower compartment contained the following offerings:

pinasa (the fruit known in Malay as *nangka*, often pronounced *nakka*)

atsimoen (cucumbers, called *timoen* in Malay)

pira ni manoek (hen's eggs)

halas (edible aromatic rhizomes of a relative of the ginger plant known in Malay as *langkoeas*, or *lakkoeas*)

oeras (purificatory sand, piled neatly in a mound and serving as a base for a coconut-shell cup containing the lemon water used for ceremonial purification)

Both the upper and lower compartments were neatly floored with leaves of a species of Ficus called *motoeng*,[5] in which the lower leaf surface is white. In making the flooring, called *lapik boeloeng motoeng*, the white surface is kept uppermost. It gives a very beautiful and neat effect. In front of the *langgatan* there hung from a forked stick *mange-mange ni pinang* (a betel-palm inflorescence) and from the altar itself, two bamboo water tubes *(inganan ni aek)*. Behind the *langgatan* was a *boeloeng ni bagot*, a cut frond of the sugar palm (cf. 3, p. 3; 5, Pl. XX) planted obliquely in the earth with a *mombang* (magical basketry construction, in this instance a tray) suspended from it, the latter bearing an offering of sugar cane, and in addition, small portions of all the offerings found in the lower compartment of the *langgatan*.

From Ypes (27, p. 119) we learn that the *langgatan* appears in the Dairi region, where the word is *lĕnggatĕn*, as a hanging tray on which palm sugar and grated coconut are placed at the rice-harvest ceremonies as an offering to the soul of the rice. Here it seems equivalent to the *mombang* of the Pardembanan and the *antjak* of the Malays.

---

[5] *Motoeng* leaves are also important in the chief Dairi ceremonies, and their use in Toba has previously been noted by Winkler in *Die Toba-Batak auf Sumatra* (see Ypes, 27, p. 183).

SACRED EDIFICES OF SUMATRA

NOTES ON RELATED MATTERS

UNBURIED COFFINS

In Karoland as in the other Batak districts a body is sometimes kept at the house in an elaborately decorated coffin pending the ceremonies which must precede permanent disposal of the body. Such a coffin, kept under the eaves of a house at Sĕrbakti, was opened for Adam (1); it contained a skeleton from which the flesh had disappeared. Adam's photographs are of exceptional interest in that they show the coffin to have the form of a rhinoceros bird (hornbill) with the head carved at one end and the tail at the other. The hornbill is somehow important in Batak ceremonial, being more or less interchangeable with the horse, as shown by the fact that the so-called *koeda-koeda* ("something like a horse") mask of the funeral dance (see 6, Pls. I, V) in reality represents a hornbill.

A former article (4, Pl. XV) has given a photograph and description of an unburied coffin containing the corpse of a chief in the Simeloengoen country. The custom of leaving the coffin and corpse of a chief in the house pending certain ceremonies is also found in Toba. Plate XXX shows such a coffin in the chief's house at Palianan, at the top of the mountain near Parapat. Palianan had all the appearance of a purely Toba kampong although located at the edge of the Simeloengoen country. The coffin was carved and painted with black, red, and white, but had at each end a structure resembling a bird's tail. It was roughly suggestive of a canoe as seen from the side.

EQUESTRIAN FIGURES

The writer has never been in the Dairi district northwest of Toba Lake, but has seen one of the curious graves surmounted by an equestrian statue in that part of Toba (southwest of the lake) which has been most influenced by Dairi customs (Pls. XXII–XXIII). The first illustration of such a grave was published by Van der Tuuk (16, Pl. XXI) from a sketch by Von Rosenburg, and Von Rosenburg (21, p. 61) later figured one at Lobang Tungkung in the Dairi district, stating that such images, called *hoda-hoda bakkuwang*, were more common among the Dairi than the Toba. They do not occur east of the lake, so far as the writer's observations indicate.

An interesting anonymous note (15), included without title in an administrative report and therefore likely to be overlooked, gives illustrations of the Dairi *hoda-hoda bakkuwang*. The photographs and notes are presumably by J. H. G. Schepers. At Talangalan, in the Pakpak region west of Toba Lake, on the way from Sidikalang to Dolok Sĕmponan (not far from Kampong Salak) a surveying party found a burial place with five closely grouped equestrian statues, of which two excellent illustrations are published. Since the chief at Talangalan was noncommunicative regarding them, a coolie hired at Salak gave what information was obtained. Of the five statues all but the central one had two riders, interpreted as representing a deceased chief with his principal wife in front of him. The central statue, with one rider only, is interpreted as the monument to a chief who was survived by his wife. Behind the horses was a stone bird, said by the chief of Talangalan to have no special significance and to be an ornament only. (The anonymous author suggests that it is connected with the widespread belief that a bird takes the souls of the dead to the realm of shadows.)

When a *radja* died, his body was kept six days in a coffin in the house until a funeral feast was organized. Then the coffin was placed shallowly in the ground at the burial place, the rooflike lid above the ground. When the body had decomposed, the coffin was exhumed and the remains were burned. The ashes, tied up in a white cloth, were laid in the arms of the deceased's image, or placed in a stone urn before the statue. (Only the monument with a single rider had an urn for the ashes.) When these truly remarkable monuments were discovered, on the march of the surveying party to Dolok Sĕmponan, they appeared to be entirely neglected and were so hidden by the tall grass that they could not be photographed until the return trip when the place was cleaned up. It seems, therefore, that the living pay relatively little attention to the graves. The horses were said to indicate that the deceased were chiefs.

A striking similarity of the equestrian grave carvings with smaller ones commonly found on magical apparatus in the Toba and Karo lands suggests probable similarity of purpose. Figures on horseback are often found as finials on the tiny spirit houses which are perched on the roof trees of the dwellings of important chiefs in Karoland. They sometimes form the roof apexes of the dwellings of important Karo chiefs or of the Karo *gĕritĕn* or bone houses in which bones, especially skulls, of the Karo chiefs are preserved (See Pl. XVI, Fig. 2). Similar equestrian figures are carved at the apex of the *toengkat malekat* (magic staff; in Toba, *toenggal panaloewan*), as stoppers of the containers for magical mixtures *(pĕrminakĕn)*, on sheaths and handles of swords and ceremonial knives (the upper part of the sheath being the horse and the handle being the rider), and as protective carvings in relief on the doors of granaries. Since in general the symbol most frequently associated with the mounted figure is the lizard, these two motives may be taken to symbolize the deified ancestors and the beneficent gods of field and house. It is to be supposed that when the horse was first introduced into the Batak lands it was brought by immigrants of great distinction, who presumably had the status of chiefs and magicians and in time were deified.

The riding figure at the apex of a magic staff collected by the writer for the Raffles Museum was said in Karoland to represent Si Donda Katik Oetan. In front of him, sitting on the horse's head, is a female figure, Si Bĕroe Tapian Radja Binoeasa. Other female figures, represented behind the chief rider, all represented Si Bĕroe Tiang Manik. Below the horse are figures named Goeroe Pakpak Pĕrtandang, said to be the first magicians to make a magic staff. (These legendary demigods and others were also identified in the carvings of the magic staff called the *toengkat pĕnikat*, and of some of the more elaborate *pĕrminakĕn*.) The animals carved on the *toenggal panaloewan* were the lizard (*bindaoran*, Karo) and snake (*nipe*). When the riding figure is carved on doors or walls of granaries it is associated with the lizard. The Angkola Batak have a tradition that when Gabriel blows his horn (the Angkola Batak have become Muhammadan) those who have asserted their right to a horse by breaking off a lizard's tail will be reviewed on horseback at the throne of grace. A lizard thus mutilated will become a horse at the resurrection, but will not recognize his would-be master unless he was politely addressed as Radja Odang and his pardon asked when his tail was broken off.

The association of a horseback rider with a lizard, and the almost equally frequent use of each as a motive in Batak art, would seem to indicate that some rider was particularly sacred, as we know the lizard is (6, pp. 18–20, and Pl. XIV). The lizard is the symbol of beneficent gods of soil and house, and is associated with the culture heroine who introduced mat making. Horses are presumably not indigenous to Sumatra. When first introduced centuries ago, their possession must have brought great distinction, and the first horseman would naturally have become one of the legendary heroes, and when deified would have been represented on horseback.

There are traces of horse symbolism at ceremonies and on graves far south and east of the Dairi region. The matter has been alluded to elsewhere (4, p. 49; 6, p. 10).

The equestrian grave monument illustrated (Pls. XXII–XXIII) is near the main highway from Balige to Taroetoeng, and was said by the local Batak to mark the burial place of Radja Pangalitan *marga* Namaban of Djonggi ni Hoeta. In Hoetagaloeng's fine collection of Batak pedigrees (8) the Nababan ("Namaban") line of descent is carried to Ama ni ("father of") Pangalitan, whose descendants are said to have lived at Nagasariboe, which is in the vicinity of this statue and burial mound. According to the traditions, Radja Pangalitan was the seventh in line of descent from the stem ancestor of *marga* Namaban, and the twentieth generation from the gods. A rapid search of the personal names in the Batak genealogies, in the hope of finding some that might indicate the possession of horses, turned up the name Parhoda Onggang ("Hornbill-Horse-Rider") in the same general line of descent (seventh cousins twice removed) as Radja Pangalitan, but two generations earlier. Parhoda Onggang belonged to the seventh generation descended from a certain Toga Si Hombing and to the eighteenth generation from the gods, whereas Radja Pangalitan belonged to the ninth generation from Si Hombing and twentieth from the gods. The horse is much earlier than this particular monument.

Batak graves are places of offering and supplication. The images placed upon them are tenanted by the spirits of the departed. The same idea is carried over to certain magical carvings resembling the statues on the burial places. All of these were provided with *tondi* (soul stuff) by being fed with *poepoek* (a mash made of certain parts of human sacrifices) and were tenanted by protective spirits. These were represented as chiefs on horseback. In the region west of Toba Lake the carving for an especially powerful protective spirit, whether naturally such, that is an ancestral spirit, or a captive spirit secured as a protector by means of magic, took the form of a rider, and the magical carvings spread far from the center of origin. The writer supposes that many of the older equestrian grave images originally implied the sacrifice of a horse at the grave, and that the *topeng-koeda-koeda* dance, found throughout the Batak lands, remains as the equivalent of the former sacrifice of horse and of slaves, or retainers. The dance with the horse mask spread far down into the East Coast jungle, where presumably, in the old days, there were no horses, or at least very few of them. We may be reasonably sure that in the Batak lands the horse came by way of the West Coast or the regions to the north (Atjeh), and became important (as it has remained until the present) in the high plateau around Toba Lake, where it was associated with chiefs and with ancestor worship, especially among the Dairi and Karo. It was probably in the Dairi region that the symbolism of the horse in the ancestor cult was transferred to magic or religious apparatus such as the magic staff, the receptacles for magic oil, and the masks for funeral dances. The latter apparatus spread somewhat to the lowland East Coast people who had no horses, and their ancestral graves did not have equestrian statues, which belong, quite distinctively, to the region west of Toba Lake. It has already been mentioned in connection with the discussion of the Batak coffin and funeral dances (6, p. 10) that there is a close association of hornbill and horse in Batak symbolism. Some of the ceremonial significance of the hornbill may have been taken by the horse after it was introduced.

STONE SARCOPHAGI AND GRAVESTONES SHAPED LIKE SARCOPHAGI

In addition to the stone equestrian figures which are most typical of the Dairi graves and the cross-legged, seated figures known from the Pardembanan region in Asahan, there are also stone sarcophagi in the Toba region, as well as stones, marking burial tumuli, which have the form of a sarcophagus but are solid. These structures are sphinxlike but have the form which is common to most Batak structures, and which some writers derive from a boat. It is remarked by many observers that the typical narrow Batak house with its curved roof tree has the lines of a boat. The stone monuments in question resemble a covered boat, high at prow and stern. The "prow" is a gigantic human head, called *singa* ("lion"), and the suggestion given by the structure is that it may have some relation, even if a remote one, to the Egyptian sphinx. The most impressive of these monuments were found and photographed by Tassilo Adam in the west of Samosir, the region near Poesoek Boekit where myth locates the origin of the Batak race from the gods. Unfortunately the local traditions regarding these truly remarkable sculptures do not seem to have been recorded by any of the writers on the Batak. Mr. Adam, with the consent of the Colonial Institute of Amsterdam, has allowed me to reproduce his photograph (Pl. XXIV). The human head is called *singa*, but nevertheless has hornlike ornaments that suggest a bull (Siva's bull?) rather than any other non-human creature.

The heads on the fine monuments shown in Mr. Adam's photograph are more human than several less elaborate ones seen by the writer in the part of the Toba region south of the Lake. In Balige there are at least two similar but simpler carvings, one of which (Pl. XXVI, Fig. 1) suggests the Siva bull quite as much as or more than the lion or sphinx. The other (Pl. XXV), which appears to be the older, is distinctly human in its suggestion, and shows no horns.

The largest sarcophagus-shaped monument seen by the writer (Pl. XXVI, Fig. 2), located on a large artificial burial tumulus at Loemban Koeala, Toba, has a face so conventionalized that it is difficult to say what it suggests. Volz (19, pp. 331–353) has been more interested in Batak sculpture and symbolism than any other author, and the reader is referred to his valuable discussion of the geographical distribution and possible meaning of the *singa* and other art motives.

MODERN CONCRETE SARCOPHAGI

The only evidence of any new flowering, or even survival, of native art in the Toba region was shown a few years ago in the construction of a considerable number of concrete sarcophagi by the natives. They followed their own art forms exclusively, which seems remarkable in view of the complete collapse of their material culture, which has quickly followed contact with the white race. Toba, the former center of Batak culture, is fast becoming utterly and depressingly nondescript, as the remaining Batak houses fall into ruin and are replaced by atrocious styleless imitations of European buildings. The newer places such as Porsea, or those which have grown so rapidly that the new dominates the old, such as Balige, have little of interest for the traveler unless he has time to seek for it away from the main roads.

The recent concrete tombs to which the writer referred were built up of rubble and then plastered over with cement. Cement "lion" heads and other architectural ornaments were apparently cast (or chiseled out of cement blocks) and built into place as the surfacing with cement proceeded. One can have only admiration for the remarkably good design and execution of these structures, and for the conservation of the old artistic spirit which they show. Between 1918 and 1927 few of these new tombs seem to have been erected; and some of those that antedate 1918 have suffered at the hands of vandals. It is seldom that one has an opportunity to see what effect the introduction of an entirely unfamiliar material (such as concrete), requiring a new technique in working, will have on the art expression of a primitive people. These concrete tombs show very conclusively that, in spite of the disintegrating effect of European contact, the Batak retained for a time the capacity for development of their own peculiar art through the adoption of materials and technical processes from outside. It appears that the movement to create a new art in the spirit of the past was abortive. The forces bringing about cultural disintegration are too strong. These few pictures of the concrete tombs (Pls. XXVII–XXIX) may already, therefore, have an antiquarian interest.

REFERENCES

1. ADAM, TASSILO, Battak Days and Ways. Asia, XXX (1930), 118–125.
2. ANDERSON, JOHN, Mission to the East Coast of Sumatra in MDCCCXXIII under the Directions of the Government of Prince of Wales Island. Edinburgh and London: W. Blackwood, 1826.
3. BARTLETT, H. H., The Manufacture of Sugar from *Arenga saccharifera* in Asahan, on the East Coast of Sumatra. Ann. Rep. Mich. Acad. Sci., XXI (1920), 155–165.
4. ———— The Grave-Post (*Anisan*) of the Batak of Asahan. Papers Mich. Acad. Sci., Arts, and Letters, I (1923), 1–58, pls. I–XXV.
5. ———— The Labors of the *Datoe:* Part I. An Annotated List of Religious, Magical, and Medical Practices of the Batak of Asahan. *Ibid.*, XII (1930), 1–74, pls. I–XXX.
6. ———— The Labors of the *Datoe:* Part II. Directions for the Ceremonies. *Ibid.*, XIV (1931), 1–34, pls. I–XX.
6ª. BOURLET, P. A., Funérailles chez les Thay. Anthropos, VIII (1913), 40–46, plate.
7. HAGEN, B., Rapport über eine im Dezember 1883 unternommene wissenschaftliche Reise an den Toba-See. Tijds. Ind. Taal-, Land-, en Volkenkunde, XXXI (1886), 328–382.
7ª. HERNSHEIM, FRANZ, Südsee-Erinnerungen (1875–1880). Berlin: A. Hofmann und Comp., [1883].

8. HOETAGALOENG, W. M., Poestaha taringot toe tarombo ni Bangso Batak. Lagoeboti, 1926.
9. JOUSTRA, M., Batakspiegel. Uitgaven van het Bataksch Instituut, No. 3, Leiden: Van Doesburgh, 1910.
10. JUNGHUHN, FRANZ, Die Battaländer auf Sumatra. Zweiter Theil. Völkerkunde. Berlin: G. Reimer, 1847.
11. KERN, H., De Fidji-taal vergeleken met hare verwanten in Indonesië en Polynesië (Verbeterd en bijgewerkt) (1886). Verspreide Geschriften's-Gravenhage: Mart. Nijhoff, IV, 243–343; V (1916), 1–141.
11ª. KUBARY, J. S., Ethnographische Beiträge zur Kenntnis des Karolinen Archipels. Leiden: P. W. M. Trap, 1895. (See Plates XXXIII–XXXIX for illustrations of shrines.)
12. MAASS, ALFRED, Durch Zentral-Sumatra. 2 vols. Berlin: B. Behrs, 1910.
12ª. MATSUMURA, AKIRA, Contributions to the Ethnography of Micronesia. Journ. Coll. Sci. Tokyo Imp. Univ., XL (1918), Article 7, 1–174, pl. I–XXXVI.
13. NEUMANN, J. H., Karo-Bataksche Offerplaatsen. Bijdr. Taal-, Land-, en Volkenkunde v. Ned.-Ind., LXXXIII (1927), 514–551.
14. PLEYTE, C. M., Bataksche Vertellingen. Utrecht: H. Honig, 1894.
15. [SCHEPERS, J. H. G.], De hoffd- en secundaire Driehoeksmeting van de Residentiën Oostkust van Sumatra, Tapanoeli, Riouw en Djambi. Jaarverslag van den Topographischen Dienst in Nederlandsch-Indie over 1914, pp. 15–28. Batavia, 1915.
16. VAN DER TUUK, H. N., Bataksch-Nederduitsch Woordenboek. Amsterdam: F. Muller, 1861.
17. VAN HASSELT, A. L., Volksbeschrijving van Midden-Sumatra. Leiden: E. J. Brill, 1882.
18. Ethnographische Atlas van Midden-Sumatra, met verklarenden Tekst. Leiden: E. J. Brill, 1881.
18ª. VERGOUWEN, J. C., Het Rechtsleven der Toba-Bataks. 's-Gravenhage: Mart. Nijhoff, 1933.
19. VOLZ, W. T. A. H., Nord-Sumatra. Band I, Die Batakländer. Berlin: D. Reimer, 1909.

20. VON BRENNER, J. FREIHERR, Besuch bei den Kannibalen Sumatras. Würzburg: L. Woerl, 1894.
21. VON ROSENBERG, H., Der Malayische Archipel. Leipzig: G. Weigel, 1878.
22. WAITZ, THEODOR, Anthropologie der Naturvölker. Leipzig: F. Fleischer, 1859–77.
23. WARNECK, J., Tobabataksch-Deutsches Wörterbuch. Batavia: Landsdrukkerij, 1906.
24. Die Religion der Batak, ein Paradigma für die animistischen Religionen des indischen Archipels. Göttingen: Vandenhoech und Ruprecht, 1909.
25. Das Opfer bei den Tobabatak in Sumatra. Archiv. f. Religionwissensch., XVIII (1915), 333–394.
26. WILKINSON, R. J., A Malay-English Dictionary. Singapore [etc.]: Kelly and Walsh, Ltd., 1901–3.
27. YPES, W. K. H., Bijdrage tot de Kennis van de Stamverwantschap, de inheemsche Rechtsgemeenschappen, en het Grondenrecht der Toba- en Dairibataks. 's-Gravenhage: Mart. Nijhoff, 1932.

PLATES I-XXXI, WITH
DESCRIPTIONS

PLATE I

PLATE I

Parsoeroan (temple) and the strongly stockaded *parhordjaan* (sacred inclosure) at Ihat Pane, Asahan. The people of this place have entered Islam, and have allowed animals to destroy the sacred plants. Probably the structure no longer exists, since this photograph dates from 1918.

PLATE II

Underneath the *parsoeroan* at Ihat Pane, Asahan. The platform is a resting place for spirits. The lower jaw and horns of the water buffalo remain from the initial sacrifices at the dedication of the *parsoeroan*.

PLATE II

PLATE III

PLATE III

Parhordjaan (ceremonial inclosure) and *parsoeroan* (temple) at Boentoe Pane, Asahan. In the old days Boentoe Pane was one of the important little pagan "kingdoms" of the Pardembanan Batak, but it has now been reduced to insignificance. The cannibal feasts at this place over a century ago were described by Anderson (2). Some of the *kabosaran* (insignia) of his pagan forebears were still in the possession of the Radja in 1918. The inclosure at Boentoe Pane was open to animals, but had the hanging fringe of palm leaves over the entrance which prevented the ingress of evil spirits.

PLATE IV

The *andjapan* (altar) beside the *parsoeroan* at Boentoe Pane. It is of much simpler construction than one of those previously illustrated (5, pl. V), but has the essential features: (1) a lower offering place, set off by a fringe of shredded palm leaves; (2) the platform for the main offerings; (3) the tall posts at the front corners, where hang the inflorescence and half-ripe infructescence of the *pining* (betel-nut palm); and (4) the two bamboos split at the top and splayed into *parpagaran* (conical receptacles for containing special offerings). It lacks the *boeloeng ni bagot*, which would almost certainly be set up anew for each ceremony.

PLATE IV

PLATE V

PLATE V

Detail of the *parsoeroan* at Boentoe Pane, showing especially one of the two carved *naga* (mythical snake) heads which are represented with a curious excrescence under the throat. On the front wall is a painting of a tiger; along the side an elephant, a cobra, and a water buffalo (the latter not showing in the photograph).

PLATE VI

The *parhordjaan* (sacred inclosure), *porlak ni debata* ("garden of the gods"), and *parsoeroan* (temple) at Radja Meligas, Tano Djawa, Simeloengoen.

PLATE VI

PLATE VII

Fig. 1

Fig. 2

PLATE VII

FIG. 1. *Parsoeroan* (temple) within permanent *parhordjaan* (ceremonial inclosure) at Radja Meligas, Tano Djawa, Simeloengoen. The plants within the inclosure are dedicated to the gods. Among them the *pining* (betel-nut palm) and pepper vine are most prominent, but there are also the red-leaved *Cordyline fruticosa* and variegated-leaved Codiaea of several sorts.

FIG. 2. Datoe Goenoeng standing beside the *batoe paranggiran* (sacrificial stone) in the ceremonial inclosure at Goenoeng Meligas, Tano Djawa, Simeloengoen (1918).

PLATE VIII

FIG. 1. Underneath the *parsoeroan* at Radja Meligas, shown in Plate VII. The benches are said to be resting places for spirits. The gongs are used only for ceremonies, and the horns are those of the water buffaloes sacrificed at the dedication of the *parsoeroan*.

FIG. 2. The *parhordjaan* (ceremonial inclosure) and *parsoeroan* at Goenoeng Meligas, Tano Djawa, Simeloengoen.

PLATE VIII

Fig. 1

Fig. 2

PLATE IX

Fig. 1

Fig. 2

PLATE IX

FIGS. 1–2. Views of the *djoro* ("spirit house") of "Pati Lebanus *marga* Pangariboean, *mate* [deceased] 9 Augustus 1926," near Balige, Toba. The curious structure on the ridge of the roof suggests a boat or possibly a bird. At the front is a human figure. At the center is an image representing *manoek-manoek* (some sort of bird). Each wall of the *djoro* has crude pictures painted upon it, some purely magical and others apparently in substitution for offerings. The mound outside the inclosure is an old burial tumulus planted with lemon grass.

PLATE X

Fig. 1. One of the drawings on the wall of the *djoro* shown in Plate IX. It represents things which it is hoped the spirit may be able to use: at the top, a *soeling* (flute); upper left, a sugar-palm tree and implements for collecting palm juice for wine or sugar-making; upper right, the always useful domestic fowl; middle, a blunderbuss (of which a good many examples still remain in the Batak lands), for defense; below, a net for fishing.

Fig. 2. Paintings on the *djoro* shown in Plate XI. Nothing can be made of some of the figures, but others represent a sugar palm, horses, a fowl, fish, and a dog (for food).

PLATE X

Fig. 1

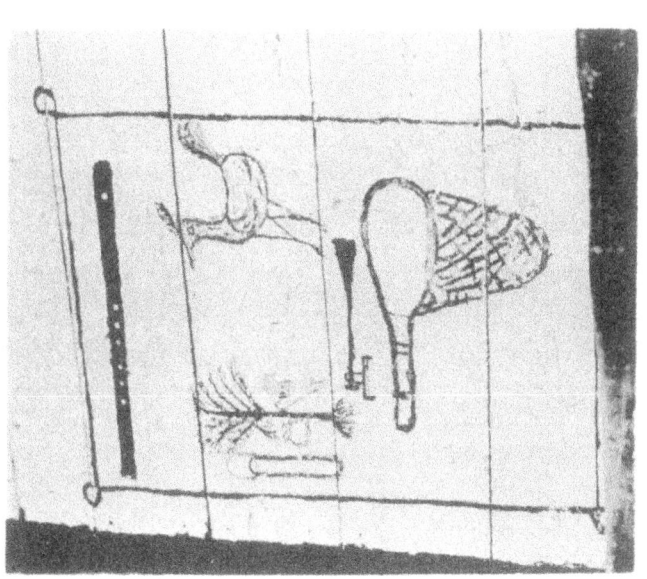

Fig. 2

PLATE XI

Fig. 2

Fig. 1

PLATE XI

FIGS. 1–2. Two views of a *djoro* at Loemban Silambi, near Parsambilan Djaë, Toba. The architecture here resembles that of the *djoro* shown in Plate IX; it is the less typical form. The resemblance of the roof to a boat is very striking. The birds, presumably representing protectors of the spirit, have curious forward extending appendages which seem to represent a second position of the wings, and to indicate that the birds are in flight.

PLATE XII

FIGS. 1–2. Two views of a typical *djoro* at Tangga Batoe, near Balige, Toba. The ceremonial inclosure still persists. This structure was nicely made, with good wood carvings exactly like those of a dwelling house and with a painted (red, white, and black) frieze. The post at the middle of the roof suggests somewhat vaguely the grave-post (*anisan*) of Asahan (4), also the *barotan* (sacrificial post) which is seen in the larger Toba boats, but most of all the spirit ladder shown on the Simeloengoen coffin (4, Pl. XV).

PLATE XII

Fig. 1

Fig. 2

PLATE XIII

PLATE XIII

Djoro at Porsea, Toba. The one at the left of the sacred *hariara* tree was especially ornate, well carved, and painted, and altogether worthy of a detailed study which there was no time to make. The figure at the front of the gable and the curious tail-like structure at the back suggest the Toba boat. The intermediate figures are the *manoek-manoek* (birds) so familiar as protective devices in Toba magic and religion, and in old days as characteristic of the dwelling house architecture as of the spirit houses.

PLATE XIV

Roof of the second *djoro* shown in Plate XIII (at the right of the *hariara* tree). The four birds (*manoek-manoek*) are tied with long cords to the figure at the front (or prow, if the gable here represents a boat). Most of the *djoro* seen had this same feature.

A book by Vergouwen (18[a]), just received as this article goes to press, has a reference (p. 83) to earlier illustrations of the *djoro* and also of the modern cement grave monument (called *"simen,"* from "cement") in a work that quite escaped the attention of the writer: D. W. N. de Boer, "Het Toba-Bataksch huis," *Meded. Encycl. Bureau*, afl. XXIII. Vergouwen states that the *djoro* of Toba Holboeng (the district bordering the southern end of Toba Lake and extending eastward) is built according to recent custom on the grave of a childless person, whose spirit is of negligible importance, whereas a *"simen"* is built as the home of a spirit who will grow in importance as the number of his descendants increases.

PLATE XIV

PLATE XV

Fig. 1

Fig. 2

Fig. 3

PLATE XV

Fig. 1. Typical *djerat* of the Simeloengoen Batak of Tano Djawa. Photographed at Kampong Riah na Poso, 1927. This structure has the same general resemblance to the Simeloengoen house that the Toba *djoro* has to the Toba house. The *djerat* in Tano Djawa always has under it *anisan* (grave-posts) quite like those which are commonly used in Asahan without the *djerat*, a structure which is very rare in Asahan. Under each *djerat* in Tano Djawa one usually finds a pair of posts of the forms which in Asahan are used separately to indicate male and female burials, but which in Tano Djawa are found on the same grave.

Figs. 2–3. The two grave-posts under the *djerat* shown in Figure 1. One (Fig. 2) is of the form which in Asahan would be male, ending in a water bottle, whereas the other (Fig. 3) ends in a bowl and miniature house, and would in Asahan indicate a female burial. Either the sex distinction is not observed in Tano Djawa, or a single *djerat* is used for more than one burial.

Kubary (11[a]) found in the Palau Islands and illustrated with beautiful plates not only diminutive shrines showing much similarity to the *parsoeroan*, but also still smaller ones strikingly like the "female" type of Batak *anisan* in that they had the form of a post with a miniature house carved at the apex. The *djerat* of Simeloengoen would appear from a plate published by Bourlet (6[a]) to have an almost exact counterpart in Anam.

PLATE XVI

Fig. 1. *Djerat pajoeng* in *pĕndawanĕn* (burial inclosure) at Gadja, Karoland. More ornate than the *djerat* of the East Coast lowlands (i.e. Simeloengoen and Asahan), even as the house architecture is correspondingly more ornate, it has for finial a *pajoeng* (umbrella) and at the ends of the four gables the horns of the water buffaloes sacrificed and eaten at the funeral feast. The sacred plants, *kalindjoehang* (red-leaved *Cordyline*) and lemon grass, are grown abundantly around the *djerat*, the former showing against the lower slope of the roof. In Karoland, the first funeral, when the body is placed under the *djerat*, may or may not be followed by exhuming and cleaning the skull for preservation in the *gĕritĕn*, depending upon rank and *mĕrga* of the deceased.

Fig. 2. *Gĕritĕn* (ossuary) at Kaban Djahe, Karoland. In this house are placed the skulls of the ancestors after a preliminary burial of the bodies has made it possible for them to be cleaned and adorned for preservation. Note the sacred inclosure (the picture dates from 1918) which was later (by 1927) allowed to fall into disrepair, but would doubtless be replaced on the occasion of new ceremonies. An interesting story of events connected with this *gĕritĕn* is told by Adam (1). The reader will observe that the finial is an equestrian figure, a frequent art motive in religious and magical structures.

PLATE XVI

Fig. 1

Fig. 2

PLATE XVII

PLATE XVII

Pantangĕn ("forbidden place") at the foot of Dĕlĕng Koetoe ("Louse Mountain") near Kampong Goersinga, Karoland. This is the only Karo *pantangĕn* known to the writer. It is the inclosure where Goeroe na Bolon was photographed (6, Pls. IV–V) in the costumes of the *topeng-koeda-koeda* dance.

PLATE XVIII

Fig. 1. *Běběren* ("place for making offerings") at Kampong Raja, Karoland. It is one which has been newly established or repaired, and contains only small plants. It was found in the same village in which the usual square type is also to be seen. Note on the right a bamboo joint set firmly in the earth, to serve, with a corresponding one on the inside, as a style by which to enter the *běběren* when an *andjap-andjap* (altar) is to be set up or furnished with offerings.

FIG. 2. *Běběren* in one of the semi-wild gardens in the outskirts of the village of Raja, Karoland. It contains a Ficus tree, an Areca palm, a pepper vine, plants of banana, and *kalindjoehang* (*Cordyline*). The same garden in which this *běběren* was located contained also a stone *pangoeloebalang*, similar to those illustrated in a former article (6, Pl. X), the function of which was to guard the fruits and vegetables.

PLATE XVIII

Fig. 1

Fig. 2

PLATE XIX

Fig. 1

Fig. 2

PLATE XIX

FIG. 1. *Běběren* ("place for making offerings") at Kampong Gadja, Karoland. This sacred inclosure contained for the most part *kalindjoehang* (a red-leaved ornamental variety of *Cordyline fruticosa*), which is by far the most important ceremonial plant of the Karo Batak.

FIG. 2. *Běběren* at Kampong Raja, Karo Plateau. Note the banana plants, dedicated to the spirits, and the pole with an offering of maize ears. On this pole some of the maize ears of the new crop are hung to dry just as the bulk of the harvest is hung, on large frames, elsewhere in the village. The drying frames for maize are one of the conspicuous features of each Karo village.

PLATE XX

FIG. 1. *Běběren* ("place for making offerings") at Kampong Kěling, Karo Plateau. It is the small square inclosure at the left side of the picture, containing plants of banana and *kalindjoehang* (*Cordyline*), and a small three-legged altar. The small structures in the middle and right foreground are granaries. On the platforms under them the women and girls gather to weave cloth and mats.

FIG. 2. *Pěrsěmbahěn* (cleft wand made of palm stem, in which is placed a *sirih* leaf as an offering to spirits) photographed at the summit of Dělěng Baroes, Karoland. Several of these offerings were set up by the writer's native companions to propitiate mountain spirits who might have been annoyed by the disturbance caused by botanizing! The *pěrsěmbahěn* is identical with the Dairi *pěnalěpěn*, mentioned by Ypes (27).

PLATE XX

Fig. 1

Fig. 2

PLATE XXI

PLATE XXI

Andjap-andjap (temporary altar) of the Karo Batak, erected on the crater rim at the summit of Děleng Sibajak. The offerings consist of a coconut and *sirih* leaves, with the other constituents for betel chewing. The altar itself has three legs, made of two-pronged sticks, which support a lattice of sticks on which a covering of leaves is placed. The three slender upright sticks at the left of the altar are *pěrsěmbahěn* (cleft wands), each of which holds a *sirih* leaf.

PLATE XXII

Burial tumulus and equestrian statue of Radja Pangalitan *marga* Namaban, at Djonggi ni Hoeta, near the main highway between Balige and Taroetoeng (see also 15, with a fine plate showing similar graves). Note the Ficus trees (called *haoe hariara*), which are planted at burial sites, and are then esteemed as sacred to the spirits. Descendants of a stem forefather are buried, if possible, at a place where cuttings of the original *hariara* are planted, and the Batak are able to give the line of descent of the sacred trees just as they know the descent of the chiefs buried under them. If the author may venture a guess, it is that the sacred banyan trees of the Batak lands derive their name from Hari and Hara—Vishnu and Siva (*haoe hariara*, "tree of Vishnu and Siva").

PLATE XXII

PLATE XXIII

PLATE XXIII

Equestrian grave image of Radja Pangalitan *marga* Namaban, at Djonggi ni Hoeta between Balige and Taroetoeng. The statue has been recently painted by the natives, so that details such as jacket and bridle have no antiquarian significance.

PLATE XXIV

Stone sarcophagi of the Toba Batak on the west side of the Island of Samosir, photographed by Tassilo Adam and reproduced by kind permission of the Colonial Institute of Amsterdam. The sarcophagus on the right has an obviously detachable lid. The one on the left appears from the photograph to be a solid monolith, the ossuary proper in this instance being the large stone urn in front of it. Adam found these structures filled with skulls, presumably those of the chiefs, cleaned for preservation in the sarcophagus or urn after the preliminary burial or laying away of the corpse in a coffin kept in the house (see Pl. XXX and 4, Pl. XV; also 1, text fig.).

These great Toba sarcophagi are interesting as showing no trace of the horse motive. The general form might be interpreted as houselike or boatlike (every architectural form of the Batak has the upwardly curved ridge line) and the great sphinxlike head is exactly that which occurs as the chief among the carvings on the front of the traditional Toba house. As a house carving it is called *takal singa* ("lion charm") or *singa ni roema* ("lion of the house"). The name, of course, indicates that part of the Batak had ancient origin from, or contact with, people who had some tradition of the lion, an animal which the Batak have even less reason to know, except by tradition, than the Cingalese, who derive their name from it. Study of the varying forms of the *singa* or *sinha* as an art motive in India, Ceylon, and Persia might enable the geographical distribution and focus of one of the old cultural waves which reached Indonesia to be traced. The sphinxlike Batak lion of these Samosir graves has nothing in common with the doglike Chinese lion, the tradition of which reached China overland by way of Central Asia, whereas the Batak lion tradition must have reached Sumatra by way of the coast of India.

PLATE XXIV

PLATE XXV

Fig. 1

Fig. 2

PLATE XXV

FIGS. 1–2. Two views of an ancient sarcophagus at Balige, Toba, said to belong to Radja Pangabing *marga* Pardede. This monumental carving, although in bad repair, shows the same essential features as the sarcophagi photographed on Samosir by Adam (Pl. XXIV). The *marga* Pardede is one of the well-known Toba families, but the position of Radja Pangabing in the line of descent from the stem ancestor is not shown by Hoetagaloeng (8) or Ypes (27).

PLATE XXVI

Fig. 1. The gravestone of Radja Djoeara Monang *marga* Siahaan, at Balige, Toba. The genealogical tables of Hoetagaloeng (8) place Radja Djoeara Monang in the fifteenth generation from the gods, and in the second generation from the stem ancestor of the *marga* Siahaan (a grandson). This monument would appear to be recent as compared with that shown in Plate XXV.

Fig. 2. An ancient monolithic gravestone shaped like a sarcophagus, located on a burial tumulus at Sitorang Paraloangin, Pandjaitan Sitorang, Loemban Koeala, Toba. It is known as the Batoe ni Djai Hoetan ("Stone of the Forest Lord"). Djai Hoetan is said to have been one of the early chiefs of the *marga* Pandjaitan at Sitorang, but his place in the genealogy is not indicated by Hoetagaloeng (8). The most massive of the ancient stones seen by the writer.

PLATE XXVI

Fig. 1

Fig. 2

PLATE XXVII

PLATE XXVII

Modern concrete tombs at Balige, Toba. These follow very closely the tradition of the old stone sarcophagi. The one on the right is interesting in that to some extent it shows the lines of the Toba house, having imitations in concrete of the great timbers which terminate in the sphinxlike *"singa ni roema."*

PLATE XXVIII

Figs. 1–2. The most artistic of the cement tombs near Balige. If the lower chamber is hollow, the construction is probably mechanically defective, but the artistic effect as seen from the side (Fig. 1) is very good. The *singa* heads are well executed, and the scroll ornamentation of the "tail" end of the ridge is very well proportioned and graceful.

PLATE XXVIII

Fig. 1

Fig. 2

PLATE XXIX

PLATE XXIX

A modern concrete tomb at Tangga Batoe, near Balige, Toba. This tomb is interesting in that there have been incorporated into the modern composition various older stone carvings, two of the *singa ni roema*, the *pangoeloe-balang* (cf. 5, Pls. XVI–XVII) in front, and the curious phallic (?) stones. Part of the stones are of the form which some writers, perhaps correctly, would interpret as the *yoni*, whereas the others are the *lingga*. (See discussion of this matter in an earlier paper, 4, pp. 50–52.)

PLATE XXX

Coffin of a dead Toba chief, kept in the house at Kampong Palianan, on the mountain near Parapat. Hanging from the gallery are the five smaller drums, which always constitute the set beaten on great ceremonial and festive occasions (cf. 4, Pl. VII), together with a large one, at the left. Drumming and playing of the *saroene* (see 5, Pl. XXX) are all-important in Batak ceremonies, since certain beats and tunes (*lagoe*) are used to summon the spirits. As noted in the text, the ceremonial summoning of the spirits by drumming at the sacred inclosure is believed to have been retained by the Muhammadan Malays of Central Sumatra, after they had been converted from paganism, as the call to prayer, which is certainly an anomaly in Islam.

PLATE XXX

PLATE XXXI

PLATE XXXI

Sketch explaining the Batak (Pardembanan) *andjapan* (altar) made in 1918 for the writer before he had seen one. It is interesting as an example of the drawing of an unschooled native (Bidin *marga* Sirait Holboeng of Silo Maradja, Asahan). He has labeled the *datoe* (priest); the *boeloeng hotang bane* (rotan leaves forming the superstructure); the *toenggal panaloewan* ("magic staff,"— near the ladder); the *tanggah debata* ("ladder of the gods," with its notches upside down, as they are always made, since certain spirits are upside down); the *boenga sijala* "of which the Malay name is *palang*" (the tall, massive, clublike inflorescences of *Phaeomeria magnifica*, a member of the ginger family, shown at the side of the altar); and *boeloeng ni bagot* (the graceful tail-like frond of the sugar palm, *Arenga saccharifera*, which is interpreted as the pathway of those spirits who arrive at the altar from the air). The whole drawing is labeled *andjapan tempat makan debata* ("the altar, eating place of the gods").